D0805689

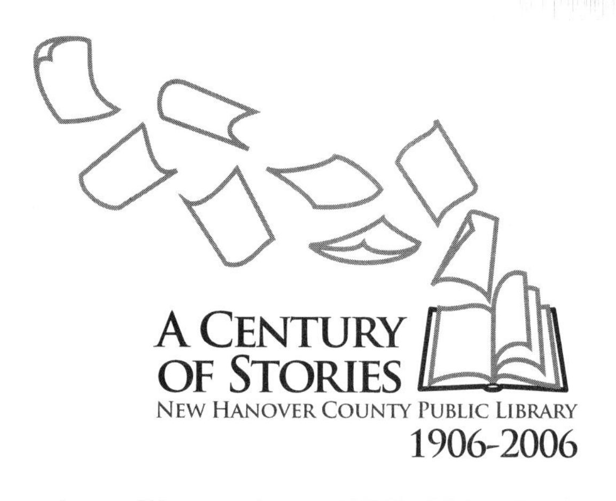
A CENTURY
OF STORIES
NEW HANOVER COUNTY PUBLIC LIBRARY
1906-2006

Living on the Plains

By Allan Fowler

Consultant
Linda Cornwell, Coordinator of School Quality
and Professional Improvement
Indiana State Teachers Association

Children's Press®
A Division of Grolier Publishing
New York London Hong Kong Sydney
Danbury, Connecticut

Visit Children's Press® on the Internet at:
http://publishing.grolier.com

Designer: Herman Adler Design Group

Library of Congress Cataloging-in-Publication Data

Fowler, Allan.
Living on the plains / by Allan Fowler; consultant, Linda Cornwell.
p. cm. — (Rookie read-about geography)
Includes index.
Summary: An introduction to the Great Plains and prairie areas of the United States.
ISBN 0-516-21565-5 0-516-27054-0 (pbk.)
1. Human geography—Great Plains Juvenile literature. 2. Prairie ecology—Great Plains Juvenile literature. 3. Plains—Great Plains Juvenile literature. [1. Prairies. 2. Prairie ecology. 3. Ecology. 4. Great Plains.] I. Title. II. Series.
GF504.G74F68 2000
910`.02145—dc21 99-30440
CIP

Printed in the United States of America.
1 2 3 4 5 6 7 8 9 10 R 09 08 07 06 05 04 03 02 01 00

Long ago, glaciers, which are huge sheets of ice, moved over the land.

A glacier

The glaciers left many areas that are flat with few trees. This flat land is called a plain.

Some plains are not completely flat. They have low, rolling hills.

Rolling plains

A map of the plains areas of the United States and Canada

Plains cover much of the central United States and Canada. In the United States, the plains lie between two great mountain systems.

They are the Appalachian (a-puh-LAY-shun) in the east and the Rockies in the west.

The plains are split by the Mississippi River.

The part of the plains east of the Mississippi River is called the prairie.

West of the Mississippi, the plains are called the Great Plains.

Mississippi River

Bison

At one time, the only people who lived on the plains were American Indians. They shared the land with huge herds of bison, or buffalo.

Then great numbers of people began coming from the east. Many traveled in covered wagons, pulled by oxen or horses.

A family on a covered wagon

St. Louis, Missouri

The grassy plains became
a land of farms, towns,
and villages.

Some of the towns grew into
big cities, such as Chicago,
Illinois, St. Louis, Missouri,
and Topeka, Kansas.

Today, much of the plains is farmland.

The land is good for farming because the glaciers left rich soil.

Fields of wheat or corn spread out for miles.

A field of wheat

Machines like this one
gather the wheat crops.
You eat wheat in bread,
cereal, and pasta.

In some parts of the plains, there isn't enough rainfall for farming.

But the grass grows well enough for cows and sheep to eat. This is called grazing.

Sheep grazing

A farmer works his field using a plow pulled by two horses.

When farmers first
moved to the plains,
life was very hard.

Families had to grow all
of their own food. Many
made their own clothing.

Farmers worked their fields
by hand. They often used
horses to pull their plows.

Today a farm family's life
is much different.

Machines like tractors make
farming faster and easier.

People can get their food
at grocery stores. They
can buy their clothing at
shopping malls.

A tractor

But life on the plains
isn't always easy.

Winter days are often
freezing. Summers are
very hot.

Storms called tornadoes
can destroy houses.

A tornado strikes a small town.

Despite difficulties, people who live on the plains have developed a way of life that is best for their surroundings.

GEHL

Words You Know

bison

covered wagon

glacier

machinery

Mississippi River

plain

tornado

Index

About the Author

Allan Fowler is a freelance writer with a background in advertising. Born in New York, he now lives in Chicago and enjoys traveling.

Photo Credits

©:Archive Photos: 22 (DeWitt Historical Society), 13, 30 top right (Lambert); Dembinsky Photo Assoc.: 17 (Darrell Gulin), 21 (Emilio Mercado); Landslides Aerial Photography: 9, 14, 31 top (Alex S. MacLean); Photo Researchers: 25, 30 bottom right (Richard Hutchings), 3, 30 bottom left (Fred McConnaughey), 10, 30 top left (Tom McHugh), 5, 31 bottom left (Rod Planck), 18 (Earl Roberge); The Image Works: cover (Cameramann), 29 (Crandall); Tony Stone Images: 27, 31 bottom right (Alan R. Moller).

Map by Bob Italiano.